湯姆和蘇菲上學了

Tom and Sofia start School

Henriette Barkow

Priscilla Lamont

CHINESE & ENGLISH

Touch the arrow with the TalkingPEN to start

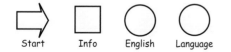

Start   Info   English   Language

湯姆和蘇菲上學了

Tom and Sofia start School

Henriette Barkow
Priscilla Lamont

Chinese translation by Sylvia Denham

mantra lingua

湯姆　　我的新老師來我們的家，她的名字是羅老師，她為我和媽媽
　　　　拍了一張照片，我跟著為她畫了一幅圖畫，羅老師說我上學時，
　　　　我的圖畫便會掛在課室的牆上。

Tom　　　My new teacher came to my home. Her name is Miss Ross. She took a photo
　　　　of me and my mum. Then I did a drawing for her. Miss Ross said that my
　　　　picture will be on the classroom wall when I start school.

蘇菲　　媽媽帶我和安娜去購物，她說我們需要購買特別的衣服以便上學時穿，我買了體操用的帆布鞋和襪子，安娜買了新皮鞋，因為她需要鞋。安娜覺得上學真好。

Sofia　　Mum took me and Anna shopping. She said we had to get special clothes for school. I got plimsolls for PE and new socks. Anna got new shoes 'cause she needed them. Anna said school is cool.

The night before

蘇菲　　安娜說我的老師羅老師**很可愛**。
　　　　我將我所有的衣服放好，讓我在早上能夠很快便準備好上學，
　　　　媽媽說我們不能遲到。

Sofia　　Anna said that my teacher Miss Ross is *love-e-ly*.
　　　　I put out all my clothes so I can get ready quickly in the morning.
　　　　Mum said we mustn't be late.

湯姆　阿德不想上學，我告訴媽媽阿德認爲他會迷失的，媽媽說阿德
　　　會沒事的，並說阿德會認識很多好像蘇菲、安娜和我的人。
　　　我告訴阿德我會照顧他的。

Tom　　Ted doesn't want to go to school. I told Mum that Ted thinks he'll get lost.
Mum said Ted will be OK. She said Ted will know lots of people like Sofia
and Anna and me. I told Ted I'll look after him.

The BIG day

湯姆　　爸爸帶我和阿德上學去。爸爸說
　　　　他記得他上學的第一天，他怎可能
　　　　記得很多很多年以前發生的事呢？

Tom　　Dad is taking me and Ted to school.
　　　　Dad said he can remember his first
　　　　school day. How can he remember
　　　　something that happened years and
　　　　years and years ago?

蘇菲	我已準備好了，安娜還在綁她的鞋帶，但我想現在就去，我不想遲到。媽媽說安娜，快呀。安娜，快呀，我想現在就去！
Sofia	I'm ready to go and Anna is not. She is doing her laces but I want to go now. I don't want to be late. Mum said hurry up Anna. Hurry up Anna, I want to go NOW!

On the way to school

| 蘇菲 | 媽媽打開門，安娜和我衝下樓梯，在樓梯的下面，我看到湯姆和他的爸爸。 |

| Sofia | Mum opened the door and Anna and me raced down the stairs. At the bottom we saw Tom and his Dad. |

湯姆　　蘇菲、安娜和她們的媽媽、還有我和爸爸、以及阿德
　　　　一直行到學校，我握著爸爸的手。安娜說上學真好。

Tom　　Sofia and Anna, and their mum and me, and Dad and Ted walked
　　　　all the way to school. I held Dad's hand. Anna said school is cool.

The school

湯姆　　當我們抵達學校時，有一名女士等著，
　　　　她問我的姓名。我說湯姆，她說她的名字
　　　　是布林太太。阿德躲在我的口袋裏。

Tom　　When we got to school there was a woman waiting.
　　　　She asked my name. I said Tom. She said her name
　　　　was Mrs Plum.
　　　　Ted hid in my pocket.

蘇菲　　　當我們抵達學校時，校長正在等候著，她跟所有的新生
　　　　　打招呼，安娜說她這樣做是讓我們都感到受歡迎。

Sofia　　　When we got to school the head teacher was waiting.
　　　　　She came to say hello to all the new children.
　　　　　Anna said she does it to make us feel welcome.

Our class

蘇菲   媽媽帶我到我的課室，羅老師就在那裏，還有
       一個成年人叫占姆。我有我自己的掛鉤，那是用來
       掛我的外套和體育袋的。媽媽說了聲再見，
       揮著手走出門口。

Sofia   Mum took me to our class. Miss Ross was there. And a grown-up
        called Jim. I got my own peg. That's for my coat and PE bag.
        Mum said bye. She waved as she went out of the door.

湯姆　爸爸帶我到我的課室，我讓爸爸看我的圖畫。我告訴爸爸說阿德感到憂慮。爸爸說阿德會沒事的，因爲他有我，而我又有阿德。爸爸給我一個擁抱後便說等會兒見，我跟著也說再見。

Tom　　Dad took me to our class. I showed Dad my picture. I told Dad Ted was worried. Dad said Ted would be OK because Ted had me. And I had Ted. Dad gave me a hug. He said see you later. I said bye.

First lesson

湯姆　　羅老師點名登記，她說她每天都會點名登記，
　　　　她叫我們的名字時，我們便要說聲到。

Tom　　Miss Ross called the register. She said
　　　　every day she will call the register.
　　　　She said we have to say yes when
　　　　she calls our name.

蘇菲　　　羅老師說我們有很多事情要做，她說做事情會很有趣。我們第一件要做的事是玩名字遊戲，我認識到很多名字，莎拉是我的朋友。

Sofia　　Miss Ross said we had lots of jobs to do. She said doing jobs is fun. Our first job was to play the name game. I know lots of names. Zara is my friend.

Morning break

蘇菲　　　羅老師說現在是小息，我們不出去玩，我們都喝水和吃水果。
　　　　　我坐在莎拉和莉莉旁邊。

Sofia　　　Miss Ross said now it's break time. We don't go out to play. We get a drink
　　　　　of water and fruit. I sat next to Zara and Lili.

湯姆　　小息時，我們可以去廁所。羅老師說**洗手**和記得**關水龍頭**。

Tom　　At break time we can go to the toilet. Miss Ross said WASH YOUR HANDS.
　　　　Miss Ross said remember to TURN OFF THE TAPS.

湯姆　　　尚恩坐在我的旁邊，我希望尚恩喜歡我。
　　　　　「你好！」尚恩說，他說他喜歡我的圖畫。

Tom　　　Sean sat next to me. I hope he likes me. "Hello!" said Sean.
　　　　　He said he liked my picture.

蘇菲　　羅老師拿了我們的圖畫，貼在牆上，我則在一張有我的名字的卡上填上顏色，然後放在抽屜上。

Sofia

Miss Ross took our pictures and put them on the wall. Then I coloured a card with my name to put on my drawer.

Lunch time

蘇菲　　　鐘響了，它的聲音很響亮！我們要洗手和排隊。莎拉握著
　　　　　我的手，她吃學校午餐，和我一樣。

Sofia

A bell rang. It made a BIG noise! We had to wash
our hands and line up. Zara held my hand.
She has school dinners like me.

午膳時間

| 湯姆 | 尚恩吃自備午餐，跟我一樣，我們都有午餐盒。我們走到大禮堂，那裏很**吵鬧**。我們坐在長檯旁。我有乳酪、麵包、一個蘋果和果汁。 |

| Tom | Sean has packed lunch like me. We got our lunch boxes. We went to the BIG hall. It was very NOISY. We sat at long tables. I had cheese and bread and an apple and juice. |

Playtime

湯姆　　尚恩、利奧、阿迪和我玩捉迷藏，長凳是家。
　　　　阿德一直在我的口袋裏。

Tom　　　Sean and Leo and Adi and me played tag. The bench was home.
　　　　　Ted hid in my pocket.

蘇菲　　莎拉、莉莉和我玩跳繩，莉莉跌倒，傷了膝蓋，需要藥用膠貼，
　　　　莉莉說傷口不痛，莉莉真是勇敢。

Sofia　　Zara and Lili and me played skipping. Lili fell over and hurt her knee.
　　　　It needed a plaster. Lili said it doesn't hurt. Lili is very brave.

Story time

蘇菲　　我們都坐在地毯上，老師為我們閱讀一本很大的書內的故事。

Sofia　　We all sat on the carpet. Miss read us a story from a BIG book.

湯姆　　讀完故事後，我們一起玩拍手遊戲，我們更學了一首歸家的詩歌。

Tom　　At the end of the story we played a clapping game. We learnt a going home rhyme.

Packing up time

湯姆	羅老師說是時候回家了，我們將我們所有的東西放進抽屜裏，阿迪的抽屜在上面，我們都排隊跟著。
Tom	Miss Ross said, home time. We put all our things in our drawers. Adi has the top drawer. Then we had to line up.

蘇菲　　　羅老師說是時候取外套了，我們都走到我們的掛鈎。
　　　　　羅老師說在走廊上**不可以跑**！她看來似乎有點惱怒，
　　　　　我們便步行回課室去。

Sofia　　Miss Ross said, time to get your coats. We ran to our pegs. Miss Ross said,
　　　　　NO RUNNING in the corridor! She looked cross. We walked back to class.

Home time

蘇菲　　媽媽和安娜來到我的課室，我讓她們
　　　　看我畫的圖畫，羅老師和占姆說再見，
　　　　我也向莎拉和莉莉說再會。

Sofia　　Mum and Anna came to my class. I showed them
　　　　my picture I painted. Miss Ross and Jim said bye.
　　　　I said bye to Zara and Lili.

湯姆	在歸家時間時，媽媽和爸爸來到課室，我有**很多**關於尚恩、利奧和阿迪的事要告訴他們，還有我做了的所有事。爸爸說我現在已經是一個長大的學生了！
Tom	At home time Mum and Dad came to the classroom. I had sooo much to tell about Sean and Leo and Adi and all the jobs I had to do. Dad said I was a big schoolboy now!

湯姆　　　我結識了很多朋友，尚恩是我的朋友，還有阿迪和利奧。尚恩是我最要好的學校朋友，阿德則是我家中最要好的朋友。阿德喜歡學校，他想再去。

Tom　　　I made lots of friends. Sean is my friend. And Adi and Leo. Sean is my best school friend. Ted is my best home friend. Ted likes school. He wants to go again.

蘇菲　　　安娜、媽媽和我吃了蛋糕，安娜有功課要做，我沒有功課。媽媽說莎拉可以在星期五放學後來我們的家。安娜說得對 － 上學真好。

Sofia　　　Anna and Mum and me had cake. Anna had homework. I don't have homework. Mum said Zara can come after school on Friday. Anna was right – school is cool.

If you have found this book helpful, there are three more titles in the series that you may wish to try:

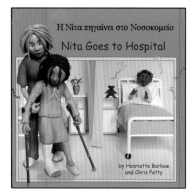

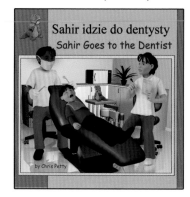

Nita Goes to Hospital
Sahir Goes to the Dentist
Abi Goes to the Doctor

You might like to make your own car, furnish your own house or try out some clothes in the "My...series" CD Roms

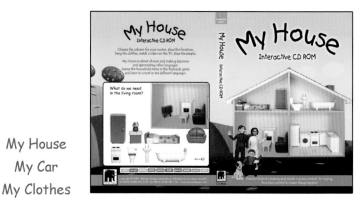

My House
My Car
My Clothes

You may wish to welcome parents and carers in 18 languages with the Welcome Booklet CD Rom Series where you can publish key information about your school - photos, policies, procedures and people:

Welcome Booklet to My School
Welcome Booklet to My Nursery
All About Me!

First published in 2006 by Mantra Lingua Ltd
Global House, 303 Ballards Lane
London N12 8NP
www.mantralingua.com

Text copyright © 2006 Henriette Barkow
Illustration copyright © 2006 Priscilla Lamont
Dual language copyright © 2006 Mantra Lingua Ltd

A CIP record for this book is available from the British Library

Tom and Sofia start School

The first day at school is an enormous step for every child.
Tom is worried. Will he get lost in his new school? Will he make any friends?
Sofia is excited and can't wait to go to big school like her sister.
Join Tom and Sofia on their first school day.

Tom and Sofia start School is part of **Mantra's First Experience** series.
Other titles in the Series:
Nita Goes to Hospital
Sahir Goes to the Dentist
Abi Goes to the Doctor

Tom and Sofia start School is available in 26 dual language editions:
English with Albanian, Arabic, Bengali, Chinese, Farsi, French, German,
Greek, Gujarati, Hindi, Italian, Japanese, Kurdish, Malayalam, Panjabi,
Polish, Portuguese, Russian, Simplified Chinese, Somali,
Spanish, Tagalog, Tamil, Turkish, Urdu or Vietnamese.

ISBN 978-1-84444-564-6

9 781844 445646 >

mantra lingua

Chinese & English